Ravensology Trivia Challenge

Baltimore Ravens Football

Ravensology Trivia Challenge

Baltimore Ravens Football

Researched by Al Netzer

Tom P. Rippey III & Paul F. Wilson, Editors

Kick The Ball, Ltd
Lewis Center, Ohio

Trivia by Kick The Ball, Ltd

College Football Trivia

Alabama Crimson Tide	Auburn Tigers	Boston College Eagles	Florida Gators
Georgia Bulldogs	LSU Tigers	Miami Hurricanes	Michigan Wolverines
Nebraska Cornhuskers	Notre Dame Fighting Irish	Ohio State Buckeyes	Oklahoma Sooners
Oregon Ducks	Penn State Nittany Lions	Southern Cal Trojans	Texas Longhorns

Pro Football Trivia

Arizona Cardinals	Baltimore Ravens	Buffalo Bills	Chicago Bears
Cleveland Browns	Dallas Cowboys	Denver Broncos	Green Bay Packers
Indianapolis Colts	Kansas City Chiefs	Minnesota Vikings	New England Patriots
New Orleans Saints	New York Giants	New York Jets	Oakland Raiders
Philadelphia Eagles	Pittsburgh Steelers	San Francisco 49ers	Washington Redskins

Pro Baseball Trivia

Atlanta Braves	Baltimore Orioles	Boston Red Sox	Chicago Cubs
Chicago White Sox	Cincinnati Reds	Detroit Tigers	Houston Astros
Los Angeles Dodgers	Milwaukee Brewers	Minnesota Twins	New York Mets
New York Yankees	Philadelphia Phillies	Saint Louis Cardinals	San Francisco Giants

College Basketball Trivia

Duke Blue Devils	Georgetown Hoyas	Indiana Hoosiers	Kansas Jayhawks
Kentucky Wildcats	Maryland Terrapins	Michigan State Spartans	North Carolina Tar Heels
Syracuse Orange	UConn Huskies	UCLA Bruins	

Pro Basketball Trivia

Boston Celtics	Chicago Bulls	Detroit Pistons	Los Angeles Lakers
Utah Jazz			

Visit **www.TriviaGameBooks.com** for more details.

This book is dedicated to our families and friends for your unwavering love, support, and your understanding of our pursuit of our passions. Thank you for everything you do for us and for making our lives complete.

**Ravensology Trivia Challenge: Baltimore Ravens Football;
First Edition 2011**

Published by
Kick The Ball, Ltd
8595 Columbus Pike, Suite 197
Lewis Center, OH 43035
www.TriviaGameBooks.com

Edited by: Tom P. Rippey III & Paul F. Wilson
Copy Edited by: Ashley Thomas Memory
Designed and Formatted by: Paul F. Wilson
Researched by: Al Netzer

*For information on ordering this book in bulk at reduced prices, please email us
at pfwilson@triviagamebooks.com.*

International Standard Book Number: 978-1-613320-006-3
Printed and Bound in the United States of America
10 9 8 7 6 5 4 3 2 1

Table of Contents

Dear Friend,

Thank you for purchasing our *Ravensology Trivia Challenge* game book!

We have made every attempt to verify the accuracy of the questions and answers contained in this book. However it is still possible that from time to time an error has been made by us or our researchers. In the event you find a question or answer that is questionable or inaccurate, we ask for your understanding and thank you for bringing it to our attention so we may improve future editions of this book. Please email us at tprippey@triviagamebooks.com with those observations and comments.

Have fun playing *Ravensology Trivia Challenge*!

Tom & Paul

Tom Rippey and Paul Wilson
Co-Founders, Kick The Ball, Ltd

PS – You can discover more about all of our current trivia game books by visiting www.TriviaGameBooks.com.

Book Format:

There are four quarters, each made up of fifty questions. Each quarter's questions have assigned point values. Questions are designed to get progressively more difficult as you proceed through each quarter, as well as through the book itself. Most questions are in a four-option multiple-choice format so that you will at least have a 25% chance of getting a correct answer for some of the more challenging questions.

We have even added Overtime in the event of a tie, or just in case you want to keep playing a little longer.

Game Options:

One Player -
To play on your own, simply answer each of the questions in all the quarters, and in the overtime section, if you'd like. Use the Player / Team Score Sheet to record your answers and the quarter Answer Keys to check your answers. Calculate each quarter's points and the total for the game at the bottom of the Player / Team Score Sheet to determine your final score.

Two or More Players –
To play with multiple players decide if you will all be competing with each other individually, or if you will form and play as teams. Each player / team will then have its own Player / Team Score Sheet to record its answer. You can use the quarter Answer Keys to check your answers and to calculate your final scores.

The Player / Team Score Sheets have been designed so that each team can answer all questions or you can divide the questions up in any combination you would prefer. For example, you may want to alternate questions if two players are playing or answer every third question for three players, etc. In any case, simply record your response to your questions in the corresponding quarter and question number on the Player / Team Score Sheet.

A winner will be determined by multiplying the total number of correct answers for each quarter by the point value per quarter, then adding together the final total for all quarters combined. Play the game again and again by alternating the questions that your team is assigned so that you will answer a different set of questions each time you play.

You Create the Game -
There are countless other ways of using *Ravensology Trivia Challenge* questions. It is limited only to your imagination. Examples might be using them at your tailgate or other professional football related party. Players / Teams who answer questions incorrectly may have to perform a required action, or winners may receive special prizes. Let us know what other games you come up with!

Have fun!

1) How was Baltimore's nickname chosen?

Answers begin on page 17

    A)   Baltimore's police insignia
    B)   Owner's choice
    C)   Fan contest
    D)   Named after a previous team

2) What are the Ravens' team colors?

    A)   Purple, Black and White
    B)   Purple, Black, Metallic Gold and White
    C)   Purple and White
    D)   Black, Metallic Gold and White

3) What year did M&T Bank Stadium open?

    A)   1995
    B)   1996
    C)   1998
    D)   2002

4) What year did Baltimore play its first-ever game?

    A)   1995
    B)   1996
    C)   1997
    D)   1998

5) With what team was Ravens head coach John Harbaugh's first coaching job?

    A) Western Michigan University
    B) Morehead State
    C) Philadelphia Eagles
    D) Indiana University

6) In which NFL Division does Baltimore play?

    A) AFC Central
    B) NFC North
    C) NFC South
    D) AFC North

7) What is the name of Baltimore's team song?

    A) "Ravens Fight Song"
    B) "The Baltimore Fight Song"
    C) "The Ravens are Flying"
    D) "The Raven"

8) What do many Ravens fans touch for good luck in the Unitas Plaza at M&T Bank Stadium prior to a home game?

    A) Bronze Shoe
    B) Bronze Helmet
    C) Concrete Football
    D) Original Stadium Banner

9) Who did the Ravens draft with their one and only Supplemental Draft pick in 2007?

    A) Oniel Cousins
    B) Chris Chester
    C) Terrell Suggs
    D) Jared Gaither

10) Who holds the Baltimore record for having the most punts blocked in a career?

    A) Dave Zastudil
    B) Greg Montgomery
    C) Kyle Richardson
    D) Sam Koch

11) Who scored the very first touchdown in Ravens history?

    A) Ernest Byner
    B) Vinny Testaverde
    C) Derrick Alexander
    D) Herman Arvie

12) The Cowboys have never beaten the Ravens at M&T Bank Stadium.

    A) True
    B) False

13) What position did Ravens coach John Harbaugh play in college?

    A) Quarterback
    B) Punter
    C) Defensive Back
    D) Tight End

14) Who holds the Raven record for most consecutive games with a touchdown?

    A) Ray Rice
    B) Earnest Byner
    C) Todd Heap
    D) Willis McGahee

15) Did Joe Flacco win his first-ever game as a starter for the Ravens?

    A) Yes
    B) No

16) When was the most recent season Baltimore did not play a Monday Night Football game?

    A) 1997
    B) 2000
    C) 2004
    D) 2009

17) Who was the most recent player to be inducted into the Ravens Ring of Honor?

    A) Michael McCrary
    B) Johnny Unitas
    C) Jonathan Ogden
    D) Matt Stover

18) From which college have the Ravens drafted the most players?

    A) Tennessee
    B) Miami
    C) Oklahoma
    D) Alabama

19) Who holds Baltimore's career rushing yards record?

    A) Willis McGahee
    B) Ray Rice
    C) Priest Holmes
    D) Jamal Lewis

20) How many weeks were Raven players named NFL Rookie of the Week in 2008?

    A) 2
    B) 3
    C) 5
    D) 6

21) The M&T Bank Stadium has a seating capacity more than 75,000.

    A) True
    B) False

22) What year did the Raven head first appear on Baltimore's helmets?

    A) 1996
    B) 1997
    C) 1999
    D) 2003

23) How many career wins did Brian Billick have as Baltimore Ravens head coach?

    A) 80
    B) 91
    C) 99
    D) 121

24) What year did Steve Bisciotti purchase a majority stake of the Baltimore Ravens from Art Modell?

    A) 2000
    B) 2002
    C) 2004
    D) 2006

25) Who holds Baltimore's record for passing yards in a single game?

    A) Vinny Testaverde
    B) Joe Flacco
    C) Elvis Grbac
    D) Steve McNair

26) Which Ravens player led the AFC in receiving touchdowns in 1996?

    A) Derrick Alexander
    B) Michael Jackson
    C) Floyd Turner
    D) Brian Kinchen

27) How many times has Baltimore played in the Super Bowl?

    A) 1
    B) 2
    C) 3
    D) 4

28) Where do the Ravens hold their annual training camp?

    A) Temple University
    B) Dickinson College
    C) Frostburg State
    D) McDaniel College

29) Have the Ravens ever played the Colts in the postseason?

    A) Yes
    B) No

30) How many times has a Raven had greater than 2,000 yards of total offense in a single season?

    A) 5
    B) 7
    C) 10
    D) 12

31) Who led the Ravens in sacks during the 2010 regular season?

    A) Cory Redding
    B) Terrell Suggs
    C) Ray Lewis
    D) Haloti Ngata

32) Which team has Baltimore played the most in overtime games?

    A) New York Jets
    B) Cleveland Browns
    C) Miami Dolphins
    D) Pittsburgh Steelers

33) What are the most regular-season wins the Ravens have ever had in a single season?

    A) 10
    B) 11
    C) 13
    D) 14

34) Which Raven holds the NFL record for most two-point conversions in a season?

    A) Todd Heap
    B) Jamal Lewis
    C) Chester Taylor
    D) Earnest Byner

35) How many defensive touchdowns did the Ravens have in 2010?

    A) 1
    B) 3
    C) 4
    D) 6

36) What single-season NFL record did the Ravens set in 2000?

    A) Most Shutouts
    B) Fewest First Downs Allowed, Rushing
    C) Fewest Points Allowed (16-game season)
    D) Fewest Touchdowns Allowed, Rushing

37) Who is the play-by-play announcer for the Ravens Radio Network?

  A) Stan White
  B) Scott Garceau
  C) Qadry Ismail
  D) Gerry Sandusky

38) Anquan Boldin had a better completion percentage in the Ravens' 2010 regular season than Joe Flacco.

  A) True
  B) False

39) In the lyrics of Baltimore's fight song, what is spread wide?

  A) Wings
  B) Ravens
  C) Talons
  D) Defenses

40) What is the name of the Ravens' official drum line?

  A) Baltimore's Finest
  B) Marching Ravens Drumline
  C) Baltimore Ravens Drumline
  D) The Drumming Ravens

41) How many NFL opponents have never beaten the Ravens at home?

  A) 5
  B) 8
  C) 10
  D) 16

42) Who holds Baltimore's record for receiving yards in the regular season?

  A) Qadry Ismail
  B) Derrick Mason
  C) Michael Jackson
  D) Derrick Alexander

43) Who holds the Ravens record for most passing yards in a rookie season?

  A) Joe Flacco
  B) Troy Smith
  C) Kyle Boller
  D) Chris Redman

44) How many AFC Championships has Baltimore won?

  A) 0
  B) 1
  C) 2
  D) 4

45) Which Raven holds the team's single-game rushing record?

    A) Priest Holmes
    B) Willis McGahee
    C) Bam Morris
    D) Jamal Lewis

46) Who is the only Raven to be named Super Bowl MVP?

    A) Trent Dilfer
    B) Jamal Lewis
    C) Ray Lewis
    D) Brandon Stokley

47) What is Baltimore's record for most consecutive wins at home?

    A) 8
    B) 10
    C) 12
    D) 13

48) Did Brian Billick coach another professional football team after leaving the Ravens?

    A) Yes
    B) No

49) Who holds Baltimore's record for points scored in a season?

    A) Steven Hauschka
    B) Billy Cundiff
    C) Michael Jackson
    D) Matt Stover

50) What season did the Ravens celebrate their first-ever victory over the Pittsburgh Steelers?

    A) 1996
    B) 1997
    C) 1999
    D) 2000

In 2009 Baltimore Ravens tackle Michael Oher was the subject of the major motion picture "The Blind Side." Based on the book *The Blind Side: Evolution of a Game* by Michael Lewis, the movie recounts Michael's childhood of living in foster homes and attending many different schools until being taken in by the Tuohly family. It won numerous awards, including an ESPY for Best Sports Movie and earned Sandra Bullock a Best Actress Oscar. The Ravens drafted Michael "Big Mike" Oher in the first round of the 2009 NFL Draft with the 23rd pick.

1) C – Fan contest (The name comes from the poem "The Raven" by Edgar Allan Poe. The famous poet lived and is buried in Baltimore.)

2) B – Purple, Black, Metallic Gold and White

3) C – 1998 (The stadium opened on Sept. 6, 1998, and has had several name changes until M&T Bank acquired the naming rights in 2003.)

4) B – 1996 (The Ravens defeated the Oakland Raiders 19-14 on Sept. 1, 1996.)

5) A – Western Michigan University (He was the running backs and outside linebackers coach from 1984-86 for the Broncos of WMU.)

6) D – AFC North (The Ravens share the division with the Cincinnati Bengals, Cleveland Browns and Pittsburgh Steelers.)

7) B – "The Baltimore Fight Song" (This song took the place of "Ravens Fight Song" on Aug. 25, 2010, following an online vote by Ravens fans. It's an updated version of the old "Baltimore Colts Fight Song.")

8) A – Bronze Shoe (Fans believe that touching the left shoe of a bronze statue of the legendary Baltimore Colts' quarterback Johnny Unitas brings good luck.)

9) D – Jared Gaither (The Ravens picked Gaither in the fifth round of the 2007 Supplemental Draft.)

10) C – Kyle Richardson (Richardson had five punts blocked out of 364 total punts from 1998-2001.)

11) B – Vinny Testaverde (Testaverde scored on a nine-yard run against Oakland to make the score 7-0 in the first quarter.)

12) A – True (The Cowboys have only been to M&T Bank Stadium twice and lost both times.)

13) C – Defensive Back (Harbaugh played his college football at Miami University in Oxford, Ohio.)

14) D – Willis McGahee (He scored touchdowns in seven consecutive games for the Ravens in the 2007 season.)

15) A – Yes (Flacco led the Ravens to a 17-10 victory vs. the Bengals in 2008.)

16) B – 2000 (The Ravens have appeared on MNF every season since their first appearance in 2001.)

17) D – Matt Stover (Kicker for 13 years with the Ravens from 1996-2008, he played in 207 games making 402 extra points and 354 field goals for a total of 1,464 points.)

18) C – Oklahoma (The Ravens have drafted a total of seven players from Oklahoma.)

19) D – Jamal Lewis (He gained 7,801 yards rushing on 1,822 attempts from 2000-06.)

20) A – 2 (Joe Flacco was named Rookie of the Week in Week 8 and Week 17.)

21) B – False (The official seating capacity is 71,008.)

22) C – 1999 (Due to a copyright infringement lawsuit concerning the first helmet logo, the team changed to the Raven head design in 1999.)

23) A – 80 (Billick has the most career wins as a Ravens head coach from 1999-2007.)

24) C – 2004 (After purchasing 49 percent of the Ravens in 2000, Biscotti exercised an option to buy the remaining 51 percent of the team on April 9, 2004, from Art Modell.)

25) A – Vinny Testaverde (Testaverde completed 31 of 51 passes for a team record 429 yards against the St. Louis Rams in 1996.)

26) B – Michael Jackson (Jackson recorded 14 touchdowns while catching 76 passes for 1,201 yards.)

27) A – 1 (Super Bowl XXXV in 2000)

28) D – McDaniel College (Since 1996 the Ravens have trained at McDaniel College, formerly known as Western Maryland College.)

29) A – Yes (The Ravens have played the Colts twice in the postseason, losing both games by scores of 6-15 in 2006 and 3-20 in 2009.)

30) C – 10 (Seven Ravens have had over 2,000 yards in total offense a combined 10 times, most recently Joe Flacco in 2010 with 3,412 yards on 3,622 yards passing and -210 yards rushing.)

31) B – Terrell Suggs (Suggs recorded 11 sacks during the regular season.)

32) D – Pittsburgh Steelers (Raven-Steeler games have gone into overtime four times. The Ravens are 3-1 in those games.)

33) C – 13 (The Ravens won 13 regular-season games in 2006 [13-3].)

34) A – Todd Heap (In 2003, he set the NFL record for most two-point conversions in a season with four.)

35) B – 3 (Ray Lewis, Dawan Landry and Josh Wilson each returned an interception for a touchdown in 2010.)

36) C – Fewest Points Allowed (16-game season) (In 2000, the Ravens allowed only 165 points and held opponents to only five rushing and 11 receiving touchdowns.)

37) D – Gerry Sandusky (Sandusky has been the play-by-play voice of the Ravens since 2006.)

38) A – True (Boldin completed the only pass he attempted [1.000] while Flacco was 306 of 491 [.626].)

39) C – Talons (The third line in the Ravens fight song is "So fly on with talons spread wide.")

40) B – Marching Ravens Drumline (The Drumline is part of the Baltimore Marching Ravens band, which is the largest musical organization associated with any NFL team.)

41) D – 16 (The Ravens are a combined 31-0-1 against teams that have never beaten the Ravens at home.)

42) C – Michael Jackson (In 1996, Jackson gained 1,201 yards on 76 receptions in 16 games.)

43) A – Joe Flacco (He recorded 2,971 passing yards with 14 touchdowns in 2008.)

44) B – 1 (The Ravens beat the Oakland Raiders 16-3 on Jan. 14, 2000.)

45) D – Jamal Lewis (Lewis rushed for a record 295 yards against Cleveland on Sept. 14, 2003.)

46) C – Ray Lewis (He had 11 tackles, six assists, and blocked four passes. Lewis became only the second linebacker to win the award and the first on the winning team.)

47) A – 8 (Baltimore won eight straight home games from Nov. 5, 2006, to Oct. 14, 2007.)

48) B – No (Billick entered into a broadcasting career, first with ABC Sports and later with the NFL Network.)

49) D – Matt Stover (Stover recorded 135 points in 2000 [35 field goals, 30 extra points].)

50) A – 1996 (The Ravens beat the Steelers 31-17 at home in their second meeting of 1996.)

Note: All answers valid as of the end of the 2010 season, unless otherwise indicated in the question itself.

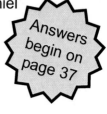

Answers begin on page 37

1) What is the name of the stadium at McDaniel College where Ravens summer training camp is held?

   A) Byrd Field
   B) Scott S. Bair Stadium
   C) Hughes Stadium
   D) Homewood Field

2) What jersey number did the Ravens' Shannon Sharpe wear?

   A) No. 69
   B) No. 72
   C) No. 77
   D) No. 82

3) When was the last time the Ravens drafted a running back in the first round of the NFL Draft?

   A) 1998
   B) 2000
   C) 2002
   D) 2007

4) Which season did Baltimore have its lowest winning percentage?

   A) 1996
   B) 1997
   C) 2005
   D) 2007

5) Does Baltimore have an all-time winning record against Pittsburgh?

  A) Yes
  B) No

6) What is Baltimore's record for most consecutive winning seasons?

  A) 3
  B) 4
  C) 5
  D) 6

7) What are the most rushing yards by the Ravens in a postseason game?

  A) 142
  B) 159
  C) 226
  D) 234

8) Where did the Ravens' General Manager Ozzie Newsome play college football?

  A) Florida
  B) Auburn
  C) Alabama
  D) Texas

9) Who holds the Ravens' record for most games in a
season with 300 or more passing yards?

    A) Eric Zeier
    B) Joe Flacco
    C) Jeff Blake
    D) Vinny Testaverde

10) Do the Ravens have a winning record in games
following a bye week?

    A) Yes
    B) No

11) All time, what are the most points the Ravens allowed in
a postseason game?

    A) 21
    B) 27
    C) 31
    D) 38

12) How many teams has Baltimore played 20 or more
times in the regular season?

    A) 3
    B) 4
    C) 6
    D) 7

13) Does Joe Flacco have the most career rushing yards by a Ravens quarterback?

  A) Yes
  B) No

14) Which opposing player gained the most yards rushing against Baltimore in a single game?

  A) James Allen
  B) Marshall Faulk
  C) Fred Taylor
  D) Terrell Davis

15) What is the M&T Bank Stadium record for longest field goal kicked by a Raven?

  A) 51 yards
  B) 53 yards
  C) 56 yards
  D) 58 yards

16) How many times has Raven free safety Ed Reed led the league in interceptions?

  A) 1
  B) 3
  C) 4
  D) 5

17) Against which team was Baltimore's first-ever NFL loss?

- A) Pittsburgh Steelers
- B) New England Patriots
- C) Houston Oilers
- D) Indianapolis Colts

18) When was the last time the Ravens had greater than 500 yards of total offense in a game?

- A) 1997
- B) 2000
- C) 2006
- D) 2009

19) How many times has Baltimore had the No. 1 overall draft pick?

- A) 0
- B) 1
- C) 3
- D) 4

20) His job at Baltimore is John Harbaugh's first head coaching position at any level.

- A) True
- B) False

21) How many yards is the longest rushing play in Baltimore history?

    A) 67
    B) 77
    C) 83
    D) 91

22) Which team has Baltimore played more than once and never beaten at home?

    A) Kansas City Chiefs
    B) New England Patriots
    C) Tampa Bay Buccaneers
    D) Carolina Panthers

23) Which opposing quarterback has played the most games against the Ravens?

    A) Ben Roethlisberger
    B) Carson Palmer
    C) Tim Couch
    D) Steve McNair

24) How many times has Baltimore played in the AFC Wild Card Playoff game?

    A) 3
    B) 5
    C) 6
    D) 8

25) The Ravens were outgained in their only Super Bowl appearance.

    A) True
    B) False

26) What year did the Ravens win their first-ever postseason game?

    A) 1996
    B) 1997
    C) 1999
    D) 2000

27) How many times has Baltimore lost a season opener played at home?

    A) 2
    B) 3
    C) 5
    D) 6

28) How many Baltimore players have been named AP NFL Defensive Rookie of the Year?

    A) 2
    B) 3
    C) 5
    D) 6

29) How many years did Jonathan Ogden play football for the Ravens?

  A) 8
  B) 9
  C) 12
  D) 13

30) How many total preseason and regular-season games did Baltimore play in its first-ever NFL season?

  A) 14
  B) 17
  C) 18
  D) 20

31) What is Baltimore's all-time longest recorded punt?

  A) 65 yards
  B) 74 yards
  C) 77 yards
  D) 80 yards

32) Do the Ravens have an all-time winning record against the AFC?

  A) Yes
  B) No

33) Who was the most recent Raven to have greater than 100 receptions in a single season?

A) Ray Rice
B) Michael Jackson
C) Derrick Mason
D) Mark Clayton

34) Who is the only Raven to have greater than 250 receiving yards in a single game?

A) Derrick Mason
B) Derrick Alexander
C) Floyd Turner
D) Qadry Ismail

35) To which team did Baltimore lose by the most points in its first NFL season?

A) San Francisco 49ers
B) Pittsburgh Steelers
C) Houston Oilers
D) Denver Broncos

36) Who was Baltimore's first-ever opponent at the M&T Bank Stadium?

A) Cincinnati Bengals
B) Jacksonville Jaguars
C) Chicago Bears
D) Pittsburgh Steelers

37) How many yards was the Ravens' longest touchdown drive in 2010?

    A) 76
    B) 85
    C) 88
    D) 93

38) Which Raven played in the most Pro Bowls?

    A) Ray Lewis
    B) Ed Reed
    C) Terrell Suggs
    D) Jonathan Ogden

39) Who holds Baltimore's record for passing yards in a season?

    A) Steve McNair
    B) Elvis Grbac
    C) Vinny Testaverde
    D) Joe Flacco

40) In 2003 the Ravens led the NFL in both rushing offense and rushing defense.

    A) True
    B) False

41) Who holds Baltimore's record for the most receptions in a single regular-season game?

    A) Priest Holmes
    B) Derrick Mason
    C) Floyd Turner
    D) Ray Rice

42) How many quarterbacks started just two games each for the Baltimore Ravens?

    A) 2
    B) 3
    C) 5
    D) 6

43) Who holds Baltimore's record for the most consecutive punts with no blocks?

    A) Sam Koch
    B) Greg Montgomery
    C) Dave Zastudil
    D) Kyle Richardson

44) How many Ravens have recorded greater than 1,000 career tackles?

    A) 0
    B) 1
    C) 4
    D) 5

45) Does Joe Flacco have greater than 10,000 career passing yards?

    A) Yes
    B) No

46) Who holds the Ravens' record for career sacks?

    A) Michael McCrary
    B) Terrell Suggs
    C) Ray Lewis
    D) Peter Boulware

47) How many Ravens had greater than 1,000 yards receiving in a single season?

    A) 2
    B) 4
    C) 5
    D) 6

48) How many opposing quarterbacks have thrown five or more touchdown passes against the Ravens in a single game?

    A) 2
    B) 3
    C) 5
    D) 7

49) How many times have the Ravens averaged 20 or more points per game in a season?

    A) 6
    B) 7
    C) 9
    D) 12

50) Who is the only Raven honored with the Bryan "Whizzer" White NFL Man of The Year Award?

    A) Matt Stover
    B) Michael McCrary
    C) Ed Reed
    D) Tony Banks

History was made in Super Bowl XXXV between the Baltimore Ravens and the New York Giants. In the third quarter, with the score 10-0 in favor of the Ravens, Duane Starks intercepted a Kerry Collins pass and returned it 49 yards for a touchdown, setting off the wildest 36 seconds in Super Bowl history. Ron Dixon of the Giants returned Matt Stover's kickoff 97 yards for a touchdown, the only Giants score of the game. On the very next kickoff Jermaine Lewis had an 84-yard return for a touchdown, making the score 24-7 Baltimore. It was the first time two kickoffs were returned for touchdowns on back-to-back kickoffs in Super Bowl history.

1) B – Scott S. Bair Stadium (Home of the Green Terror football, lacrosse and track and field teams of McDaniel College.)

2) D – No. 82 (Sharpe played two years from 2000-01 with the Ravens.)

3) B – 2000 (The Ravens drafted Jamal Lewis from Tennessee with the fifth pick of the 2000 NFL Draft.)

4) A – 1996 (The Ravens went 4-12, for a .250 winning percentage.)

5) B – No (Baltimore is 12-21 all time against the Steelers.)

6) A – 3 (2008 [11-5], 2009 [9-7] and 2010 [12-4])

7) D – 234 (In the 2009 AFC Wild Card game against the New England Patriots, the Ravens rushed for 234 yards while limiting New England to just 64 yards rushing.)

8) C – Alabama (Newsome played wide receiver for the Crimson Tide from 1974-77. In 2002, he was named general manager of the Ravens, making him the first black GM in the NFL.)

9) D – Vinny Testaverde (He passed for greater than 300 yards in a game five times in 1996.)

10) A – Yes (The Ravens are 10-5 [.667] in games after a bye week.)

11) C – 31 (The Ravens lost 24-31 to the Steelers in the 2010 AFC Divisional Playoff game.)

12) A – 3 (Cincinnati Bengals [30], Cleveland Browns [24] and Pittsburgh Steelers [30])

13) B – No (Kyle Boller holds the record for the most yards rushing for a quarterback at 440 yards. Flacco has 320 yards in just three seasons as the Ravens QB.)

14) D – Terrell Davis (In 1996, Denver running back Terrell Davis gained 194 yards on 28 carries against the Ravens.)

15) C – 56 yards (This record is held by Wade Richey. It was kicked on Sept. 14, 2003, in the second quarter of a 33-13 win against the Cleveland Browns.)

16) B – 3 (Reed led the league in interceptions with nine in 2004, nine in 2008 and eight in 2010.)

17) A – Pittsburgh Steelers (The Ravens lost 17-31 to the Steelers at Three Rivers Stadium in the second game of the 1996 season.)

18) D – 2009 (The Ravens gained 548 yards in a 48-3 win against the Detroit Lions on Dec. 13, 2009 [308 yards rushing and 240 yards passing].)

19) A – 0 (The highest draft pick the Ravens have ever had was No. 4 in both the 1996 and 1997 NFL Drafts.)

20) A – True (Harbaugh was the defensive backs coach for the Philadelphia Eagles prior to joining the Ravens.)

21) C – 83 (Ray Rice set this record on the first play from scrimmage during the 2009 Wild Card game against the New England Patriots.)

22) B – New England Patriots (The Ravens lost to the Patriots 38-46 in 1996 and again in 2007 by the score of 24-27.)

23) D – Steve McNair (He played in 15 games for the Houston Oilers/Tennessee Titans against the Ravens. McNair was traded to the Ravens and played all of 2006 and part of 2007 before retiring.)

24) C – 6 ([2000, 2001, 2003, 2008, 2009 and 2010)

25) B – False (The Ravens had 244 total yards [133 passing and 111 rushing] to the Giants' 152 total yards [86 passing and 66 rushing].)

26) D – 2000 (The Ravens beat the Broncos 21-3 in the 2000 AFC Wild Card game.)

27) B – 3 (The Ravens are 4-3 [.571] in home openers.)

28) A – 2 (LB Peter Boulware [1997] and LB Terrell Suggs [2003])

29) C – 12 (Ogden played left tackle with the Ravens from 1996-2007.)

30) D – 20 (Baltimore played four preseason games [3-1] and 16 regular-season games [4-12] in 1996.)

31) B – 74 yards (Sam Koch kicked a 74-yard punt against the Houston Texans on Nov. 9, 2008, in Reliant Stadium.)

32) A – Yes (Baltimore has an all-time record of 94-87 against the AFC for a .519 winning percentage.)

33) C – Derrick Mason (Mason caught 103 passes for 1,087 yards and five touchdowns in 2007.)

34) D – Qadry Ismail (He gained 258 yards on six receptions in a 31-24 win over the Steelers in 1999.)

35) A – San Francisco 49ers (The Ravens lost 20-38 to the 49ers at San Francisco on Nov. 17, 1996.)

36) C – Chicago Bears (This was a preseason game that the Ravens won 19-14 on Aug. 8, 1998.)

37) D – 93 (The Ravens had a 93-yard touchdown drive in the second quarter versus the Cleveland Browns on Sept. 26, 2010.)

38) A – Ray Lewis (Lewis made 12 Pro Bowl teams [1997, 1998, 1999, 2000, 2001, 2003, 2004, 2006, 2007, 2008, 2009 and 2010].)

39) C – Vinny Testaverde (He passed for 4,177 yards in 1996.)

40) B – False (The Ravens led the NFL in rushing offense [2,674 yards] but were sixth in rushing defense [1,536 yards].)

41) A – Priest Holmes (Holmes had 13 receptions for 98 yards from Eric Zeier against the Tennessee Oilers in 1998.)

42) B – 3 (Troy Smith [2007], Randall Cunningham [2001] and Scott Mitchell [1999])

43) C – Dave Zastudil (Zastudil recorded 177 consecutive punts, none blocked from Dec. 15, 2002 through Sept. 18, 2005.)

44) B – 1 (Ray Lewis has recorded 1,184 tackles since 1996. Tackles did not become an official NFL statistic until 2001.)

45) A – Yes (Flacco has passed for 10,206 yards in his career with the Ravens, since 2008.)

46) D – Peter Boulware (Boulware recorded 70 sacks in his career with the Ravens [1997-2005].)

47) B – 4 (Michael Jackson [1996], Derrick Alexander [1996 and 1997], Qadry Ismail [1999 and 2001] and Derrick Mason [2005, 2007, 2008 and 2009])

48) A – 2 (The Seahawks' Matt Hasselbeck and Steelers' Ben Roethlisberger both threw five touchdown passes in a game against the Ravens.)

49) C – 9 (1996 [23.2 points per game], 1997 [20.4 ppg], 1999 [20.3 ppg], 2000 [20.8 ppg], 2003 [24.4 ppg], 2006 [22.1 ppg], 2008 [24.1 ppg], 2009 [24.4 ppg] and 2010 [22.3 ppg])

50) B – Michael McCrary (McCrary received this award in 2000.)

Note: All answers valid as of the end of the 2010 season, unless otherwise indicated in the question itself.

1) In which year did the Ravens record their first win in Pittsburgh?

Answers begin on page 56

   A) 1996
   B) 1997
   C) 1999
   D) 2000

2) How many times have the Ravens played on a Thursday?

   A) 1
   B) 3
   C) 4
   D) 6

3) Which year was Baltimore's first-ever 10-win season?

   A) 1997
   B) 1998
   C) 1999
   D) 2000

4) How many career wins does John Harbaugh have as head coach of the Ravens?

   A) 24
   B) 28
   C) 32
   D) 35

5) What is Baltimore's largest margin of victory in a postseason game?

    A)   18 points
    B)   21 points
    C)   23 points
    D)   27 points

6) Who holds the Ravens' career record for receiving yards?

    A)   Mark Clayton
    B)   Derrick Mason
    C)   Qadry Ismail
    D)   Todd Heap

7) Which of the following Baltimore quarterbacks is the only one to throw five touchdown passes in a single game?

    A)   Tony Banks
    B)   Kyle Boller
    C)   Vinny Testaverde
    D)   Anthony Wright

8) How many combined kickoffs and punts were returned for touchdowns by the Ravens in 2010?

    A)   0
    B)   1
    C)   3
    D)   5

9) What is the Baltimore record for point after touchdowns made in a single game?

    A) 4
    B) 5
    C) 6
    D) 8

10) How many quarterbacks have the Ravens drafted in the first round?

    A) 1
    B) 2
    C) 4
    D) 6

11) Ray Lewis played in the most postseason games as a Raven.

    A) True
    B) False

12) How many career 300-yard passing games does Raven quarterback Joe Flacco have?

    A) 2
    B) 3
    C) 4
    D) 6

13) How many times has a rookie led the Ravens in sacks?

  A) 1
  B) 2
  C) 3
  D) 4

14) Who is the only Ravens defender to record nine interceptions in a single season?

  A) Chris McAlister
  B) Rod Woodson
  C) Ed Reed
  D) Ray Lewis

15) Who holds the Ravens' record for most games with 100 or more rushing yards in a career?

  A) Jamal Lewis
  B) Willis McGahee
  C) Priest Holmes
  D) Ray Rice

16) Who holds the Ravens' record for most consecutive passes attempted without an interception?

  A) Tony Blake
  B) Joe Flacco
  C) Steve McNair
  D) Eric Zeier

17) Who was the most recent Raven to record more than 150 total defensive tackles in a single season?

  A) Kelly Gregg
  B) Ray Lewis
  C) Bart Scott
  D) Ed Reed

18) What is the Ravens' record for most consecutive losses?

  A) 9 games
  B) 10 games
  C) 12 games
  D) 15 games

19) When was the last time the season-leading passer for Baltimore had fewer than 2,000 yards passing?

  A) 2000
  B) 2003
  C) 2005
  D) 2007

20) Who was the most recent non-kicker to lead the Ravens in scoring?

  A) Le'Ron McClain
  B) Jamal Lewis
  C) Willis McGahee
  D) Michael Jackson

21) What is Baltimore's all-time winning percentage at home (regular season and postseason)?

A) .488
B) .528
C) .609
D) .663

22) Has Baltimore always had official team cheerleaders?

A) Yes
B) No

23) Who was the first Raven to be inducted into the Ravens' "Ring of Honor"?

A) Peter Boulware
B) Earnest Byner
C) Michael McCrary
D) Jonathan Ogden

24) How many seasons have the Ravens gained more than 2,500 rushing yards as a team?

A) 1
B) 3
C) 4
D) 6

25) Ray Lewis was the only Raven to be named to the NFL Hall of Fame's All-Decade Team of the 2000s.

    A) True
    B) False

26) How many overtime games did Baltimore play in 2010?

    A) 1
    B) 2
    C) 3
    D) 5

27) Who is the only Baltimore player to be named NFL Offensive Player of the Year?

    A) Priest Holmes
    B) Ray Lewis
    C) Earnest Byner
    D) Jamal Lewis

28) Which Raven has the most punt returns for touchdowns in a career?

    A) B.J. Sams
    B) Jermaine Lewis
    C) Yamon Figurs
    D) Ed Reed

29) Which year did Baltimore get its 100th all-time regular-season win?

    A) 2005
    B) 2006
    C) 2008
    D) 2010

30) Who was the only non-player to be inducted into the Ravens Ring of Honor?

    A) Art Modell
    B) Rex Ryan
    C) Brian Billick
    D) Marvin Lewis

31) How many regular-season games did a Ravens running back rush for more than 100 yards in 2010?

    A) 1
    B) 2
    C) 4
    D) 5

32) What is Baltimore's longest drought between playoff appearances?

    A) 2 years
    B) 3 years
    C) 4 years
    D) 6 years

33) Against which AFC team does Baltimore have the highest all-time winning percentage (min. 3 games)?

    A) Oakland Raiders
    B) New York Jets
    C) Buffalo Bills
    D) Houston Texans

34) Who scored Baltimore's first points in Super Bowl XXXV?

    A) Matt Stover
    B) Jermaine Lewis
    C) Brandon Stokley
    D) Duane Starks

35) Has Baltimore ever failed to rush for 1,000 yards as a team in a season?

    A) Yes
    B) No

36) How many consecutive Ravens games has Jarret Johnson played in?

    A) 73
    B) 85
    C) 100
    D) 116

37) Who was the Ravens' first round pick in the 2011 NFL Draft?

    A) Jimmy Smith
    B) Tandon Doss
    C) Torrey Smith
    D) Jah Reid

38) Who holds the Ravens' record for most receptions in a career?

    A) Mark Clayton
    B) Derrick Mason
    C) Travis Taylor
    D) Todd Heap

39) How many Ravens have been inducted into the Ring of Honor?

    A) 8
    B) 10
    C) 14
    D) 16

40) When was the last season the leading rusher for Baltimore gained fewer than 700 yards?

    A) 1999
    B) 2001
    C) 2005
    D) 2008

41) When was the last time the Ravens went undefeated in the preseason?

    A) 2000
    B) 2003
    C) 2009
    D) 2010

42) What is Baltimore's all-time record for largest margin of victory?

    A) 32 points
    B) 37 points
    C) 40 points
    D) 45 points

43) How many former Raven defensive coordinators have become head coaches in the NFL?

    A) 2
    B) 3
    C) 4
    D) 5

44) What is the name of Baltimore's oldest football fan club?

    A) Council of Baltimore Ravens Roosts
    B) Baltimore Ravens Fan Club
    C) Chamber of Ravens Nests
    D) The Raven Club

45) Who scored the first touchdown for the Ravens in the 2010 AFC Wild Card Playoff game versus the Chiefs?

    A) Anquan Boldin
    B) Willis McGahee
    C) Ray Rice
    D) Todd Heap

46) Did Brian Billick win his final game as a Ravens head coach?

    A) Yes
    B) No

47) How many interceptions did the Ravens return for touchdowns in 2010?

    A) 1
    B) 3
    C) 4
    D) 5

48) How many Baltimore players had 50 or more receptions in the 2010 regular season?

    A) 1
    B) 2
    C) 3
    D) 4

49) When was the most recent season Baltimore led the NFL in field goal percentage?

    A) 2000
    B) 2006
    C) 2007
    D) 2009

50) What is Baltimore's record for most consecutive playoff losses?

    A) 3
    B) 4
    C) 5
    D) 6

The Ravens had their first-ever blocked punt and a then record setting return on Monday Night Football on Sept. 30, 2002. Ed Reed blocked the first punt in Ravens history in the second quarter against the Denver Broncos. The Ravens scored a touchdown four plays later for a 14-3 lead. Then with Baltimore leading 24-3, and only one second remaining in the first half, Denver's Jason Elam attempted a 57-yard field goal. The kick was short and Chris McAlister caught it in the end zone and returned it 107 yards for a touchdown. At the time, it was the longest play of any kind in NFL history, breaking three kickoff returns of 106 yards, the last of which was accomplished in 1979. McAlister's record was broken by the Bears' Nathan Vasher in 2005. In 2007 the Chargers' Antonio Cromartie set the current record for longest-ever play at 109 yards.

1) C – 1999 (The Ravens beat the Steelers 31-24 on Dec. 12, 1999.)

2) B – 3 (The Ravens are 0-3 all-time on Thursday games.)

3) D – 2000 (The Ravens went 12-4 finishing the season as Super Bowl Champions.)

4) C – 32 (Harbaugh is 32-16 [.667] in three seasons as Baltimore's head coach. He has the second most wins as a Ravens head coach.)

5) D – 27 points (The Ravens beat the Giants 34-7 in Super Bowl XXXV.)

6) B – Derrick Mason (Mason has gained 5,777 receiving yards since 2005.)

7) A – Tony Banks (He threw five touchdown passes in a win against the Jacksonville Jaguars 39-36 on Sept. 10, 2000.)

8) B – 1 (David Reed returned a kickoff against the Houston Texans 103 yards for the only kickoff or punt return touchdown in 2010.)

9) C – 6 (This record is shared by Billy Condiff against Detroit on Dec. 13, 2009, and Matt Stover against Green Bay on Dec. 19, 2005.)

10) B – 2 (Kyle Boller 2003 [19th pick] and Joe Flacco 2008 [18th pick])

11) A – True (Lewis has appeared in 15 postseason games as a Raven.)

12) C – 4 (He had three 300-yard passing games in 2009 and one in 2010.)

13) B – 2 (Peter Boulware [11.5 sacks in 1997] and Terrell Suggs [12 sacks in 2003])

14) C – Ed Reed (He recorded nine interceptions in 2004 and 2008.)

15) A – Jamal Lewis (Lewis had 30 games with 100 or more rushing yards from 2000 to 2006.)

16) D – Eric Zeier (Zeier threw 175 passes from Nov. 9, 1997, to Sept. 20, 1998 without an interception.)

17) B – Ray Lewis (He recorded 161 total tackles in 2003 [1,120 solo and 41 assisted].)

18) A – 9 games (The Ravens lost nine straight games from Oct. 21, 2007, to Dec. 23, 2007.)

19) D – 2007 (Kyle Boller led the team with 1,743 yards passing [168 completions on 275 attempts].)

20) C – Willis McGahee (In 2009, McGahee had 84 points on 14 touchdowns [12 rushing and two receiving] to lead the team in scoring.)

21) D – .663 Baltimore has an 81-41-1 all-time home record.)

22) B – No (The Baltimore Ravens Cheerleaders were established in 1998 as a co-ed stunt and all-female dance squad.)

23) B – Earnest Byner (He played two years as a Raven running back [1996-97] and then worked in Baltimore's front office as Director of Player Development after his retirement.)

24) A – 1 (2003 [2,674 yards])

25) B – False (In addition to Ray Lewis, the Hall of Fame Selection Committee chose Jamal Lewis, Lorenzo Neal, Jonathan Ogden and Ed Reed

26) C – 3 (The Ravens lost to the Patriots 20-23 but beat the Bills 37-34 and Texans 34-28 in overtime games in 2010.)

27) D – Jamal Lewis (Lewis received this award in 2003.)

28) B – Jermaine Lewis (He had six punt returns for touchdowns while playing for the Ravens from 1996 to 2001.)

29) C – 2008 (The Ravens beat the Raiders 29-10 at home in the seventh game of the 2008 season to record their 100th all-time win.)

30) A – Art Modell (Former owner of the Ravens, he was inducted in 2003.)

31) B – 2 (Ray Rice had two 100-yard rushing games in 2010 against the Denver Broncos [133 yards] and the New Orleans Saints [153 yards].)

32) A – 2 years (Since making the playoffs in 2000, the Ravens failed in consecutive years just once [2004 and 2005].)

33) D – Houston Texans (The Ravens have an all-time winning percentage of 1.000 [4-0] against the Texans.)

34) C – Brandon Stokley (Stokley caught a 38 yard pass from Trent Dilfer in the first quarter of Super Bowl XXXV.)

35) B – No (The fewest rushing yards as a team was 1,589 yards in 1997.)

36) D – 116 (Johnson passed Peter Boulware [113] as the all-time franchise leader in consecutive games played on Dec. 26, 2010, at Cleveland.)

37) A – Jimmy Smith (Baltimore drafted cornerback Smith out of Colorado with the 27th pick of the 2011 NFL Draft.)

38) B – Derrick Mason (Mason has recorded 471 receptions from 2005 to 2010. Todd Heap is second with 467 receptions from 2001 to 2010.)

39) C – 14 (The "Ring of Honor" encircles M&T Bank Stadium and includes five former Ravens, a former owner and eight former Baltimore Colts.)

40) B – 2001 (Terry Allen led the Ravens with 658 yards on 168 carries and three touchdowns.)

41) C – 2009 (The Ravens defeated the Redskins [23-0], Jets [24-23], Panthers [17-13] and Falcons [20-3].)

42) D – 45 points (The Ravens beat Green Bay 48-3 in 2005 and the Detroit Lions 48-3 in 2009.)

43) B – 3 (Bengals coach Marvin Lewis [1996-01], Jets coach Rex Ryan [2005-2008] and former 49ers head coach Mike Nolan 2002-04])

44) A – Council of Baltimore Ravens Roosts (The club started as a fan club for the Colts in 1957 [Council of Colts Corrals] but renamed itself in 1996 to support the Ravens.)

45) C – Ray Rice (He scored on a nine-yard pass from Joe Flacco in the second quarter.)

46) A – Yes (Billick's Ravens defeated the Steelers 27-21 in the final game of 2007.)

47) B – 3 (Josh Wilson against Houston [12 yard return], Dawan Landry [23 yard return] and Ray Lewis [24 yard return] against Carolina.)

48) C – 3 (Anquan Bolkdin [64], Ray Rice [63] and Derrick Mason [61])

49) B – 2006 (Matt Stover made 28 of 30 field goals in 2006 for a league leading percentage of .993.)

50) A – 3 (The Ravens lost their second playoff game in 2001 and then their next two [2003 and 2006].)

Note: All answers valid as of the end of the 2010 season, unless otherwise indicated in the question itself.

1) When was the most recent season a Ravens game resulted in a tie?

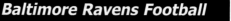

Answers begin on page 75

   A) 1997
   B) 2001
   C) 2002
   D) 2004

2) Which opponent handed Baltimore its worst defeat in 2010?

   A) New England Patriots
   B) Cincinnati Bengals
   C) Pittsburgh Steelers
   D) Atlanta Falcons

3) Who holds the Ravens' record for most punting yardage in a career?

   A) Greg Montgomery
   B) Dave Zastudil
   C) Kyle Richardson
   D) Sam Koch

4) Has a Ravens running back ever had five rushing touchdowns in a single game?

   A) Yes
   B) No

5) Which player holds Baltimore's record for most consecutive field goals made?

    A) Matt Stover
    B) Steve Hauschka
    C) Billy Cundiff
    D) Wade Richey

6) Who was the most recent quarterback to win his first regular-season game with Baltimore?

    A) Troy Smith
    B) Kyle Boller
    C) Steve McNair
    D) Joe Flacco

7) What is Baltimore's record for most consecutive years appearing in the postseason?

    A) 2
    B) 3
    C) 4
    D) 6

8) What year did the Ravens record their first shutout?

    A) 1996
    B) 1997
    C) 1999
    D) 2003

9) Against which AFC team does Baltimore have the worst all-time winning percentage (min. 3 games)?

    A) Miami Dolphins
    B) Pittsburgh Steelers
    C) Indianapolis Colts
    D) New England Patriots

10) At 38 years and 222 days of age, Randall Cunningham is the oldest person on record to play for the Ravens.

    A) True
    B) False

11) Which of the following Ravens players was not named a First Team All-Pro in 2010?

    A) Ray Lewis
    B) Haloti Ngata
    C) Billy Cundiff
    D) Ed Reed

12) When was the last season a Ravens defender had two interceptions in the same game?

    A) 2006
    B) 2007
    C) 2009
    D) 2010

13) Which Baltimore Raven recovered the most fumbles in a rookie season?

- A) Lamont Brightful
- B) B.J. Ward
- C) Terrell Suggs
- D) Dannell Ellerbe

14) Who holds Baltimore's single-season rushing yards record?

- A) Ray Rice
- B) Priest Holmes
- C) Willis McGahee
- D) Jamal Lewis

15) When was the last time the Ravens were shut out?

- A) 1996
- B) 1999
- C) 2002
- D) 2004

16) Joe Flacco passed for greater than 3,000 yards every season he has played for Baltimore.

- A) True
- B) False

17) How many times has a Raven player led the NFL in non-offensive touchdowns?

    A) 1
    B) 3
    C) 4
    D) 6

18) When was the most recent season the Ravens had two receivers with greater than 1,000 yards receiving?

    A) 1996
    B) 1999
    C) 2005
    D) 2008

19) Who holds Baltimore's records for rushing touchdowns in a game, season and career?

    A) Le'Ron McClain
    B) Ray Rice
    C) Jamal Lewis
    D) Willis McGahee

20) Which Baltimore quarterback holds the team record for highest passer rating in a single season?

    A) Steve McNair
    B) Vinny Testaverde
    C) Tony Banks
    D) Joe Flacco

21) How many total head coaches have the Ravens had in their history?

    A) 3
    B) 4
    C) 6
    D) 7

22) What is Baltimore's largest margin of victory over the Washington Redskins?

    A) 7 points
    B) 12 points
    C) 14 points
    D) 24 points

23) Who holds the Ravens record for most consecutive games with a touchdown pass?

    A) Kyle Boller
    B) Joe Flacco
    C) Tony Banks
    D) Vinny Testaverde

24) Has Baltimore played every NFL team at least once?

    A) Yes
    B) No

25) Which Raven won the Ed Block Courage Award in 2010?

    A) Ed Reed
    B) Dawan Landry
    C) Donte Stallworth
    D) Chris Carr

26) Baltimore has an all-time winning record against every AFC North opponent.

    A) True
    B) False

27) What year was the field at M&T Bank Stadium changed from natural grass to artificial turf?

    A) 2003
    B) 2005
    C) 2006
    D) 2008

28) Who was the most recent Raven to lead the NFL in yards per kickoff return?

    A) Ray Rice
    B) Jalen Parmele
    C) Le'Ron McClain
    D) David Reed

29) Who holds Baltimore's record for the most punting yards in a single season?

A) Dave Zastudil
B) Sam Koch
C) Kyle Richardson
D) Greg Montgomery

30) The Ravens were penalized for greater than 1,000 yards in 2010.

A) True
B) False

31) Which of the following is not a nickname commonly associated with the Baltimore Ravens?

A) Purple People Eaters
B) Riptide Rush
C) Death on Wings
D) Purple Pain

32) When was the last time the Ravens rushed for over 300 yards as a team?

A) 2003
B) 2005
C) 2006
D) 2009

33) When was the most recent season the Ravens gave up a safety?

    A) 2004
    B) 2006
    C) 2007
    D) 2009

34) What is the largest defeat Baltimore ever suffered in a postseason game?

    A) 14 points
    B) 17 points
    C) 21 points
    D) 27 points

35) What is Baltimore's record for consecutive regular-season wins?

    A) 5
    B) 7
    C) 8
    D) 10

36) Has Baltimore ever led the league in passing offense or total offense?

    A) Yes
    B) No

37) What year did Baltimore have a 3,000-yard passer, a 1,000-yard rusher and a 1,000-yard receiver in the same season?

    A) 1996
    B) 2000
    C) 2006
    D) 2009

38) Who was the most recent opponent to make a two-point conversion against the Ravens?

    A) Houston Texans
    B) Cleveland Browns
    C) Pittsburgh Steelers
    D) Atlanta Falcons

39) Who holds Baltimore's record for the most seasons leading the team in total sacks?

    A) Peter Boulware
    B) Michael McCrary
    C) Terrell Suggs
    D) Trevor Pryce

40) Did the Ravens travel to Miami, Fla. to play the New York Giants in Super Bowl XXXV?

    A) Yes
    B) No

41) What is the largest crowd to ever attend a Ravens home game?

    A) 71,432
    B) 72,504
    C) 73,258
    D) 76,017

42) What is the largest defeat the Ravens ever suffered on Monday Night Football?

    A) 13 points
    B) 17 points
    C) 24 points
    D) 31 points

43) Which opposing quarterback had the most 300-yard passing games against the Ravens?

    A) Kurt Warner
    B) Peyton Manning
    C) Mark Burnell
    D) Carson Palmer

44) Which Baltimore Raven had the longest interception return for a touchdown in a postseason game?

    A) Will Demps
    B) Ed Reed
    C) Chad Williams
    D) Ray Lewis

45) Who was the most recent opponent to be shut out by Baltimore?

   A) Cleveland Browns
   B) Detroit Lions
   C) Tampa Bay Buccaneers
   D) Pittsburgh Steelers

46) When was the most recent season the Ravens blocked an opponent's field goal attempt?

   A) 2006
   B) 2007
   C) 2009
   D) 2010

47) Against which team has Joe Flacco thrown the most touchdowns in his career in Baltimore?

   A) Houston Texans
   B) Pittsburgh Steelers
   C) Cincinnati Bengals
   D) Cleveland Browns

48) Who holds Baltimore's record for the most consecutive games with an interception?

   A) Ed Reed
   B) Eric Turner
   C) Rod Woodson
   D) Chris McAlister

49) Who holds Baltimore's career postseason rushing yards record?

    A) Terry Allen
    B) Ray Rice
    C) Jamal Lewis
    D) Willis McGahee

50) Against which NFL Division does Baltimore have the highest all-time winning percentage?

    A) NFC East
    B) NFC South
    C) AFC West
    D) NFC West

To prevent looking beyond the next game, former Ravens head coach Brian Billick banned the word "playoffs" from his players' vocabulary. As proof of his seriousness, players actually faced a fine if they uttered the forbidden word during the 2000 NFL season. So, in place of the word "playoffs," players started using a word that was featured on the popular TV show "Seinfeld." The word was "Festivus," which quickly caught on, even appearing on the stadium's screens during the only home playoff game that year. A scene from Seinfeld showing Cosmo Kramer saying "A Festivus Miracle!" played during the AFC Wild Card game between the Ravens and Broncos. The players and media soon began referring to the Super Bowl as "Festivus Maximus."

1) A – 1997 (The Ravens tied the Eagles 10-10 on Nov. 17, 1997, when both teams missed field goal attempts in overtime.)

2) C – Pittsburgh Steelers (Baltimore lost to the Steelers by seven points [31-24] in the Divisional playoff game.)

3) D – Sam Koch (He recorded 17,587 yards on 402 punts, for an average of 43.7 yards per punt.)

4) B – No (The most touchdowns in a game by a running back are three [Jamal Lewis two times and Willis McGahee once].)

5) A – Matt Stover (Stover made 36 straight field goals from Oct. 31, 2005 to Nov. 19, 2006, before missing a 42-yarder against the Atlanta Falcons.)

6) D – Joe Flacco (Flacco beat the Bengals 17-10 on Sept. 7, 2008, in his first game with the Ravens.)

7) B – 3 (The Ravens have appeared in the postseason during the last three years [2008, 2009 and 2010].)

8) C – 1999 (Baltimore defeated Cincinnati 22-0 at home on Dec. 26, 1999.)

9) D – New England Patriots (The Ravens have an all-time record of 1-6 against the Patriots, for a .143 winning percentage.)

10) B – False (Matt Stover was the oldest to play for the Ravens at 40 years and 326 days old.)

11) A – Ray Lewis (Lewis was named 2nd Team All-Pro.)

12) D – 2010 (Ed Reed had two interceptions in the same game three times in 2010, against Buffalo, Cleveland and Cincinnati.)

13) C – Terrell Suggs (Suggs recovered four fumbles during his rookie season of 2003.)

14) D – Jamal Lewis (Lewis gained 2,066 yards on 387 carries in 2003.)

15) C – 2002 (The Ravens lost at home to the Tampa Bay Buccaneers 0-25.)

16) B – False (In 2008, Flacco threw for 2,971 yards as a rookie. He threw for 3,613 yards in 2009 and 3,622 yards in 2010.)

17) A – 1 (Baltimore's free safety Ed Reed and Green Bay's free safety Nick Collins tied with an NFL-leading three touchdowns each in 2008.)

18) A – 1996 (Michael Jackson [1,201 yards] and Derrick Alexander [1,099 yards])

19) C – Jamal Lewis (Lewis recorded 45 touchdowns from 2000-06, 14 touchdowns in 2003 and once had three touchdowns in a game [a team record shared with Willis McGahee].)

20) D – Joe Flacco (Flacco set the team record in 2010 with a passer rating of 93.6. He ended the season with 306 completions on 489 attempts [.626], 25 touchdowns, 10 interceptions and 3,622 yards.)

21) A – 3 (T. Marchibroda, B. Billick and J. Harbaugh)

22) C –14 points (The Ravens beat the Redskins 24-10 at home on Dec. 7, 2008.)

23) D – Vinny Testaverde (He threw a touchdown pass in 13 straight games from Dec. 1, 1996 to Nov. 2, 1997.)

24) A – Yes (The Ravens have played every team at least three times each.)

25) C – Donte Stallworth (This award is given to a player from each team who exemplifies and displays courage. The team voted to give the award to Stallworth for coming back from a broken foot he experienced in a preseason game.)

26) B – False (The Ravens have an all-time winning record against Cincinnati [16-14, .533] and against Cleveland [17-7, .708], but a losing record against Pittsburgh [12-21, .364].)

27) A – 2003 (Natural grass was replaced with Sportexe Momentum Turf in 2003, which was replaced with Field Turf, another artificial turf, in 2010.)

28) D – David Reed (Reed led the NFL in 2010 with 29.3 yards per kick return, on 21 returns for 616 yards.)

29) C – Kyle Richardson (He had a total of 4,355 yards on 103 punts in 1999.)

30) B – False (Penalized 90 times for 673 yards)

31) A – Purple People Eaters (This was the Minnesota Vikings defensive line nickname of the 1970s. All others listed are nicknames that have been associated with the Ravens.)

32) D – 2009 (The Ravens rushed for 308 yards on 40 carries versus the Detroit Lions on Dec. 13, 2009.)

33) C – 2007 (DB Michael Coe of the Indianapolis Colts blocked a Sam Koch punt, the football went out of the end zone for a safety.)

34) B – 17 points (The Ravens lost two postseason games by 17 points, 3-20 to Indianapolis on Jan. 16, 2010, and 10-27 to Pittsburgh on Jan. 20, 2002.)

35) C – 8 (The Ravens won the last seven games of 2000 and the first game of 2001.)

36) B – No (1996 was the closest the Ravens were to leading the league when they ranked second in passing offense [3,978 yards] and third in total offense [5,723 yards].)

37) D – 2009 (Joe Flacco passed for 3,613 yards, Ray Rice rushed for 1,339 yards and Derrick Mason had 1,028 receiving yards in the same season.)

38) A – Houston Texans (Houston's Jacoby Jones caught a Matt Schaub pass for a successful two-point conversion late in the fourth quarter to tie the game 28-28. The Ravens won the game in overtime on an interception for a touchdown by Josh Wilson.)

39) C – Terrell Suggs (Suggs has led the team in sacks in five out of the last eight years, 2003 [12], 2004 [10.5], 2007 [5], 2008 [8] and 2010 [11].)

40) B – No (Super Bowl XXXV was played at Raymond James Stadium in Tamp Bay, Fla. on Jan. 28, 2001.)

41) A – 71,432 (This record was set on Dec. 19, 2010, in a game against the New Orleans Saints.)

42) D – 31 Points (The Ravens lost 7-38 at the Steelers in 2007.)

43) C – Mark Burnell (Jacksonville's Burnell had seven 300-yard passing games against the Ravens from 1996-2001.)

44) B – Ed Reed (Reed intercepted a Chad Pennington pass in the second quarter and returned it 64 yards for a touchdown in a 2009 Wild Card game win at Miami [27-9].)

45) A – Cleveland Browns (The Ravens beat the Browns 16-0 on Nov. 16, 2009.)

46) C – 2009 (Kelly Gregg of the Ravens blocked a 32-yard attempt by the Bengals' Shayne Graham in a 14 - 17 loss on Oct. 11, 2009.)

47) D – Cleveland Browns (Flacco has thrown eight touchdown passes in five career games against the Browns.)

48) B – Eric Turner (Turner recorded five straight games with an interception from Oct. 27, 1996 to Nov. 24, 1996.)

49) C – Jamal Lewis (Lewis gained 426 yards on 130 carries in six postseason games from 2000-07.)

50) A – NFC East (Against the NFC East the Ravens are 10-3-1 for a .750 winning percentage [3-0 against the Cowboys, 3-1 against the Giants, 1-1-1 against the Eagles and 3-1 against the Redskins].)

Note: All answers valid as of the end of the 2010 season, unless otherwise indicated in the question itself.

1) How many career touchdown passes does Joe Flacco have for the Ravens?

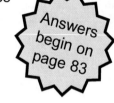

Answers begin on page 83

   A) 41
   B) 45
   C) 52
   D) 64

2) What is the Ravens' longest winning streak in the Baltimore-Pittsburgh series?

   A) 2
   B) 3
   C) 5
   D) 6

3) How many Ravens have been selected to five or more Pro Bowls?

   A) 3
   B) 5
   C) 6
   D) 8

4) Baltimore has the highest postseason winning percentage in the NFL.

   A) True
   B) False

5) What is the name of the Ravens' current costumed mascot?

    A) Edgar
    B) Raven
    C) Allan
    D) Poe

6) What was the largest halftime deficit the Ravens overcame to win a game?

    A) 11 points
    B) 14 points
    C) 16 points
    D) 21 points

7) How many times has Baltimore won six or fewer games in a season?

    A) 1
    B) 3
    C) 4
    D) 5

8) What year did the Ravens have the most First-Team All-Pro selections?

    A) 2000
    B) 2003
    C) 2008
    D) 2010

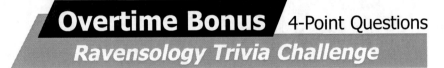
9) How many touchdown drives of 80 yards or more did the Ravens have in the 2010 regular season?

A) 6
B) 8
C) 10
D) 13

10) What is Baltimore's record for most points scored by both teams in a single game?

A) 79 points
B) 81 points
C) 85 points
D) 89 points

1) D – 64 (Flacco has thrown 64 TDs from 2008-10.)

2) B – 3 (Baltimore won their second game of 2005 and both games in 2006.)

3) A – 3 (Ray Lewis [12], Jonathan Ogden [11] and Ed Reed [7])

4) B – False (Baltimore is currently tied for third out of 32 NFL teams for all-time postseason winning percentage [9-6, .600].)

5) D – Poe (Mascots Edgar and Allan retired after the 2008 season.)

6) C – 16 points (Trailing 7-23 at halftime to the Jacksonville Jaguars, the Ravens scored 32 points in the second half to win 39-36 on Sept. 10, 2000.)

7) D – 5 (1996 [4-12], 1997 [6-9-1], 1998 [6-10], 2005 [6-10] and 2007 [5-11])

8) B – 2003 (Ray Lewis, Jonathan Ogden, Chris McAlister and Jamal Lewis.)

9) D – 13 (Baltimore's longest drive was 93 yards against Cleveland in Week 3.)

10) C – 85 points (The Ravens beat the Seahawks 44-41 in overtime on Nov. 23, 2003.)

Note: All answers valid as of the end of the 2010 season, unless otherwise indicated in the question itself.

Player / Team Score Sheet

Name:_____

First Quarter			Second Quarter			Third Quarter			Fourth Quarter			Overtime Bonus	
1		26		1		26		1		26		1		26		1	
2		27		2		27		2		27		2		27		2	
3		28		3		28		3		28		3		28		3	
4		29		4		29		4		29		4		29		4	
5		30		5		30		5		30		5		30		5	
6		31		6		31		6		31		6		31		6	
7		32		7		32		7		32		7		32		7	
8		33		8		33		8		33		8		33		8	
9		34		9		34		9		34		9		34		9	
10		35		10		35		10		35		10		35		10	
11		36		11		36		11		36		11		36			
12		37		12		37		12		37		12		37			
13		38		13		38		13		38		13		38			
14		39		14		39		14		39		14		39			
15		40		15		40		15		40		15		40			
16		41		16		41		16		41		16		41			
17		42		17		42		17		42		17		42			
18		43		18		43		18		43		18		43			
19		44		19		44		19		44		19		44			
20		45		20		45		20		45		20		45			
21		46		21		46		21		46		21		46			
22		47		22		47		22		47		22		47			
23		48		23		48		23		48		23		48			
24		49		24		49		24		49		24		49			
25		50		25		50		25		50		25		50			
___x 1 = ___			___x 2 = ___			___x 3 = ___			___x 4 = ___			___x 4 = ___	

Multiply total number correct by point value/quarter to calculate totals for each quarter.

Add total of all quarters below.

Total Points:_____

Thank you for playing *Ravensology Trivia Challenge*.

Additional score sheets are available at:
www.TriviaGameBooks.com

Player / Team Score Sheet

Name:_____

First Quarter		Second Quarter		Third Quarter		Fourth Quarter		Overtime Bonus	
1	26	1	26	1	26	1	26	1	
2	27	2	27	2	27	2	27	2	
3	28	3	28	3	28	3	28	3	
4	29	4	29	4	29	4	29	4	
5	30	5	30	5	30	5	30	5	
6	31	6	31	6	31	6	31	6	
7	32	7	32	7	32	7	32	7	
8	33	8	33	8	33	8	33	8	
9	34	9	34	9	34	9	34	9	
10	35	10	35	10	35	10	35	10	
11	36	11	36	11	36	11	36		
12	37	12	37	12	37	12	37		
13	38	13	38	13	38	13	38		
14	39	14	39	14	39	14	39		
15	40	15	40	15	40	15	40		
16	41	16	41	16	41	16	41		
17	42	17	42	17	42	17	42		
18	43	18	43	18	43	18	43		
19	44	19	44	19	44	19	44		
20	45	20	45	20	45	20	45		
21	46	21	46	21	46	21	46		
22	47	22	47	22	47	22	47		
23	48	23	48	23	48	23	48		
24	49	24	49	24	49	24	49		
25	50	25	50	25	50	25	50		
___ x 1 = ___		___ x 2 = ___		___ x 3 = ___		___ x 4 = ___		___ x 4 = ___	

Multiply total number correct by point value/quarter to calculate totals for each quarter.

Add total of all quarters below.

Total Points:_____

Thank you for playing *Ravensology Trivia Challenge*.

Additional score sheets are available at:
www.TriviaGameBooks.com